WALKING IN THE Spirit

40 DAY DEVOTIONAL

CARLOS RIVERA

For information contact:
Carlos Rivera
P.O. BOX 13526
RICHMOND, VA 23225

⊕ www.carlosmrivera.com

▶ @CarlosMRivera

f /carlosriveraministries

First Edition: 2023
ISBN# 979-8-218-18197-0

Library of Congress Control Number: pending

1   2   3   4   5   Ａ   27   26   25   24   23
                    ANNANDALE

Dedication

This book is dedicated to my Lord and Savior Jesus Christ. Since the moment I surrendered my life to You, it's been an amazing journey.

To my beautiful wife Rosalinda, the love of my life and my best friend. To my children Alana, Gabriel, and Victor: you have enriched my life and made me such a proud father.

To Joey for serving me well with "Walking in the Spirit" and being a great assistant. To Lisa for all your early mornings with me on the program and your dedication to this project.

To my "Walking in the Spirit" family for your commitment to Christ, dedication to God's Word, and prayer every weekday morning since we began. Three years and 800 episodes later, we're still planting seeds, watering seeds, and watching God move in our lives and answering our prayers.

WALK IN THE SPIRIT AND YOU WILL NOT FULFILL THE DESIRES OF THE FLESH.

GALATIONS 5:16

Forward
by Dr. Bob Rodgers

"Whosever heeds correction gains understanding...and humility comes before honor" is a proverb for all of us (Proverbs 15:32-33).

Carlos Rivera has a unique ministry. Carlos is a man of education, refinement, and great wisdom in the ways of business and what brings success to people.

At the same time, he is streetwise and able to communicate with people of all walks of life. This includes the rich and the poor, the high and the low, men and women, bank presidents and people bound by drugs.

As you go through this 40-day devotional, you see the nuggets of wisdom that cause people to rise to another level in business, in family relations, in marriage relations, and in relationship to God.

I recommend that you read and study this book for the next 40 days. As you do, three things will happen:

1. God will speak to you and give you direction.

2. You will make more money this coming year than you did last year.

3. Your relationship with your spouse and your family will greatly improve.

Thank you, Carlos, for writing this book.

Dr. Bob Rodgers

Dr. Bob Rodgers is the Senior Pastor of Evangel World Prayer Center in Louisville, KY, with over 9,000 members.

Introduction

I want to welcome you and commend you for commencing this forty-day spiritually transformational journey. Many people want to change, but few are willing to pursue it diligently. I believe that if you read, learn, and apply the daily principles in this book, it will initiate a new and exciting course that will lead you to your destiny and begin a process of a total life renovation.

Most of us long to improve and more effectively complete God's divine assignment. There is an enhanced you that God wants to introduce you to at the end of this forty-day pilgrimage. Commit yourself for just a few minutes a day, and your transformation may not be instantaneous, but it will be incremental. A new habit isn't always easy to create, but whatever pattern you form will form you. You put in consistent effort, and God's Word will do the continual work to bring out the best in you.

Why 40?

The number forty appears in the Bible around 146 times. It usually signifies a season of testing, trials, and hardship. However, the pain and suffering experienced during these times typically lead to a major shift in a person's life and in the revelation of God's purpose.

Moses spent forty years in Pharoah's palace, then forty years in the desert as a fugitive for murdering an Egyptian guard, then forty more leading the stiffed-necked, whining, complaining, and ungrateful children of Israel out of slavery to the promised land.

We also read in the book of Jonah that for forty days, the prophet Jonah forewarned the inhabitants of Nineveh that its annihilation would be inevitable if they did not repent of their innumerable sins.

There are countless other examples in God's Word of how a forty-day process is like a surgical procedure skillfully orchestrated by God to usher in a new chapter in His plan.

I want to encourage you to begin this forty-day devotional with a heart of anticipation and expectation. The Holy Spirit will accomplish and establish a fresh renewal in your mind and a refreshing rejuvenation of His purpose. Allow God's Word to permeate your heart and let The Holy Spirit introduce you to the new you, the best you, the greater you — the you God created you to be! And always remember, "When you're walking in the spirit, you will not fulfill the desires of the flesh" (Galatians 5:16).

— Carlos M. Rivera

DAY 1

Embrace the Grace

"Each time he said, 'My grace is all you need. My power works best in weakness.' So now I am glad to boast about my weaknesses, so that the power of Christ can work through me."
– *2 Corinthians 12:9, NLT*

Paul had a *thorn in the flesh.* "Scholars have guessed his struggle to be some disease or injury; some say it was a particular temptation, while others determine the thorn in the apostle's side was an ungodly, annoying person come to distract him from the Lord's work."[1] Whatever the cause, Paul saw the persistent nuisance as ultimately beneficial. With Paul, as with us, pain is a platform for the Holy Spirit's power. That is such a powerful revelation.

Rather than focusing on the pressure or tension, ask God for the grace to manage and make the most of every circumstance. "When you change the way you look at things, the things you look at change."[2]

If you have difficult people in your life, struggle with sin, or suffer an illness, stay on your knees before the Lord. Ask the Holy Spirit to change how you see things. Problems fall out of focus when your perspective is clear.

TRUST GOD TO CHANGE
THE CIRCUMSTANCES OR
CHANGE YOU.

WALK IT OUT

Does it sometimes seem God is slow in improving your circumstances?

Embrace the message of grace and hold to this truth – sometimes, the Lord changes the situation, and sometimes He will change you. God may eliminate frustrations, or He may help you endure the aggravation.

Trust God to change the circumstance or change you.

Holy Spirit,

Help me to see my circumstances through your eyes. Romans 8:28 tells me that all things work together for my good, so help me to keep my perspective focused on Your eternal plan.

Give me the grace to endure and trust You for the things I don't understand.

In Jesus' Name, Amen.

- Write what is currently causing stress and strain. It may be a relationship or situation you have no control over.

- Ask God to reveal the good He could bring from these difficulties. Whether it be something tangible or character-building (Ex. *increased patience, learning to rely more on the Lord, etc*)

DAY 2

Peace for a Lifetime

"My son, do not forget my law, but let your heart
keep my commands; For length of days and long life
and peace they will add to you."
– *Proverbs 3:1-2, NKJV*

God's Word is so powerful; His *living* Word is life-giving and life-changing. God's Word reveals God's world, so when we understand what God says, we comprehend who He is. Everything documented in the Bible has a purpose. There are no idle sentences; pointless phrases do not exist in the Creator's vocabulary. These Holy Scriptures are the means to a long, peaceful life.

Freedom from anxiety, fear, stress, worry, and tension is available and accessible to you through the knowledge of the Word of God. When the Holy Spirit reveals the things of God through His written Word, we become empowered — our understanding becomes more than a theological education; we are filled with the wisdom of application, timing, and insight. Coupled with enemy-destroying might, those roughly 770,430 words (NKJV) are your entire toolbox, but you must properly use the right tool for the right job.

"But be doers of the Word, and not hearers only, deceiving yourselves. For if anyone is a hearer of the Word and not a doer, he is like a man observing his natural face in a mirror; for he observes himself, goes away, and immediately forgets what kind of man he was. But he who looks into the perfect law of liberty and continues in it, and is not a forgetful hearer but a doer of the work, this one will be blessed in what he does." (James 1:22-25, NKJV)

GOD'S WORD REVEALS GOD'S WORLD.

WALK IT OUT

Daily reading your Bible is the key to maintaining peace of mind. When you're feeling anxious, pause and reflect on a scripture that reminds you of God's faithfulness. Read it aloud because faith comes from hearing the living breathing Word of God (Romans 10:17).

Heavenly Father,

Help me to overcome my feeling of anxiousness, worry, and fear. Speak to me through Your Word; remind me that You have me in the palm of Your hands. Thank You, Jesus, for You are my prince of peace.

In Jesus' Name, Amen.

❧ Write down a verse or two that you can cling to in your current circumstances.

❧ Why is this verse important to you today?

DAY 3

Be Prepared, Don't Panic

"But you will not even need to fight. Take your
positions; then stand still and watch the Lord's
victory. He is with you, O people of Judah and
Jerusalem. Do not be afraid or discouraged. Go out
against them tomorrow,
for the Lord is with you!"

Very often, battles appear suddenly, without warning.
Don't panic. Refuse to lose it. Whatever you may be
facing, know that God saw it coming before it ever
showed up. Preparation takes place in His presence. If
you have consistently been still with God in prayer, you
are being made ready for what is to come. You may not
see what is ahead of you, But God sees what is around

the corner. You are not unprepared – even for the unexpected if you have placed your life in His hands.

Whatever you surrender, God will control. If there are areas you suspect you still need to submit, listen carefully to the inner voice of the Holy Spirit. Let Him speak to you. When you have times of trial, do not panic. Keep praying so you can distinguish God's voice from the noise and be sensitive to the guidance of His Spirit. When the troubles come, tune in to God's voice and wait for His direction.

Television co-host and author Michelle McKinney Hammond says, "Patience is the weapon that forces deception to reveal itself."[3]

While you wait and pray, crucial information will reveal itself. Don't be too quick to move if you have been slow in getting on your knees. Meet with God, and He will be faithful to guide your steps and lead you to your answers.

DON'T BE TOO QUICK TO MOVE IF YOU HAVE BEEN SLOW IN GETTING ON YOUR KNEES.

WALK IT OUT

Today you will encounter something that can impact your life. Take time in prayer to ensure that the Holy Spirit is the one guiding and directing your path.

Don't allow emotions to cloud your judgment. Take time to seek Godly counsel.

Heavenly Father,

Help me to trust You and not what I see or what I feel. Please give me the patience and the wisdom to allow Your Holy Spirit to guide me in every decision I make. Thank You for always leading me to victory.

In Jesus' Name, Amen.

❦ "Patience is the weapon that forces deception to reveal itself."[4] What does that quote from Michelle McKinney Hammond mean to you?

❦ What areas of your life are you willing to admit you still need to surrender?

____

____

____

____

____

____

____

____

____

____

____

____

____

____

____

____

____

DAY 4

Just Laugh

"A cheerful heart is good medicine, but a broken
spirit saps a person's strength."
– Proverbs 20:17, NLT

Amid the madness, don't forget to laugh. Sometimes life comes at us hard. Laughter releases something in us. Karl Barth, one of the most influential Christian theologians of the 20th century, said, "Laughter is the closest thing to the grace of God."[5]

When you begin to laugh, it strengthens you on the inside. Instead of turning to news networks or social media and getting saturated by negativity, change your channel. It is time to flip the message in your heart and mind. Set yourself up for joy by making a conscious effort to laugh. Proverbs says that laughter accelerates the healing process (Proverbs 17:22). When you are weak in body or spirit, be active in strengthening your mind and immune system.

Laughter has an anti-inflammatory effect that protects blood vessels and heart muscles, and gives your brain a burst of serotonin, the same brain chemical affected by many antidepressants.[6] I love it when science catches up to what God has been saying for thousands of years.

"The joy of the Lord is your strength." (Nehemiah 8:10, NKJV)

"THE JOY OF
THE LORD IS
YOUR STRENGTH."
(NEHEMIAH 8:10, NKJV)

WALK IT OUT

Be intentional about bringing funny things into your life. Reading a joke book or remembering a funny incident can help distract you from the stresses of daily life.

Today choose joy and decide no matter what comes your way, you can laugh in the face of adversity because whatever you are facing is no match for God.

Heavenly Father,

Today I choose joy. I know that behind every gray cloud, there is a silver lining. Help me to always focus on the positive things in life and not get caught up in temporary challenges. Today I will laugh because — this joy that I have, "the world didn't give it, and the world didn't take it away."[7]

In Jesus' Name, Amen.

What are a few things that make you laugh or bring you happiness?

What one thing can you do today to infuse a bit of joy into your day?

DAY 5

Put God First

"My voice You shall hear in the morning, O Lord; In the morning I will direct it to You, And I will look up."
— *Psalm 5:3, NKJV*

I know you are already spending time with God because you are committing to this devotional. Be encouraged. Take a few moments and reflect on what God is speaking, journal things down as He reveals more of Himself and His will to you each day. Invest daily into the presence of God, giving God the first bit of your day. Your Father wants to hear from you, and His Spirit desires to minister to your heart, but you must sync your schedule to your Creator's agenda and purposes.

Maybe you say, "I am just too tired and too busy. There are not enough hours in the day." Hey, I get it. We are all stretched to our breaking point. But isn't that stress a good argument *for* prioritizing God's presence? When life feels too hectic to take time with God, I am telling you, it is too demanding *not* to. We need Holy Spirit direction. We will not survive our schedules without the strength and peace of the Father. His Son knew it, as well. Before the sun came up, Jesus was meeting with His Father. Do you see the practice Jesus modeled for us? Do what He did. Don't try to do this life on your own steam. More than determination, you need a daily foundation that provides a revelation for your life.

Keep your daily appointment with God – not as a matter of ritual, but a means of renewal. And God will do great things in and through your life. Enjoy your relationship with Him, not as a sense of duty, but a source of delight.

MORE THAN
DETERMINATION,
YOU NEED A DAILY
FOUNDATION THAT
PROVIDES A REVELATION
FOR YOUR LIFE.

WALK IT OUT

If God is first in your life, He should be first in your day. Let God — not the world — set the tone for your life.

Open your Bible and let God speak to you. Take time to pray so you can talk with Him.

Making God your first conversation of the day shows Him how much you value your relationship with Him.

Heavenly Father,

Before I engage in all the responsibilities of my day, help me to put You first. Before I look at my email, text, or social media, I want to spend time with You.

Your wisdom, understanding, and divine insight is what I need more than anything else.

In Jesus' Name, Amen.

❧ Are there any activities that have become a distraction in your life — Perhaps taking up too much of your time and attention? List them below.

❧ Put a star by one activity you will commit to spending less time on this week.

DAY 6

The Blessing of Giving

"Then Abraham took a tenth of all he had captured in battle and gave it to Melchizedek. The name Melchizedek means 'king of justice,' and king of Salem means 'king of peace.'"
– *Hebrews 7:2, NLT*

Lot, Abram's nephew, and the other men, women, and children had been taken captive in battle. When Abram (Abraham) heard about it, he gathered the men from his household and embarked on a rescue mission. God gave them the victory, and they "recovered all the goods" and rescued the prisoners. After his victory, Abram gave a tenth of everything to Melchizedek, God's Great High Priest, so Melchizedek blessed him. Abram's offering was a gift of gratitude and a thankful response to divine revelation from the Lord. There was no law regarding the tithe at that time; Abram's gratitude put the principle in place before Moses ever established the precept.

Hebrews 7:17 tells us Melchizedek is a kind of Christ, meaning his existence was a foreshadowing of Jesus, our High Priest. Abram's heart was moved to show his appreciation and honor to the High Priest. I believe this is to be our heart's position when it comes to giving our tithes and offerings today — not from the pressures of the law, but the posture of love. I know from experience that God rewards that kind of honor.

The tithe is God's principle for prosperity. Our posture of gratitude opens the windows of Heaven. Remember, it all belongs to Him anyway.

"THE BASIC QUESTION
IS NOT HOW MUCH
OF OUR MONEY WE
SHOULD GIVE TO
GOD, BUT HOW MUCH
OF GOD'S MONEY WE
SHOULD KEEP FOR
OURSELVES."[8]
Jim George

WALK IT OUT

Tithing is essential to releasing the promises of God.

Being consistent and obedient to God's Word as it pertains to giving, will open your life to the riches of God's blessings and demonstrate that He is a priority in your finances.

Heavenly Father,

As I bring my tithes and offerings to You, continue to open the windows of Heaven over myself and my family.

Thank you, Lord, for abundance and overflow in every area of my life — not only to be blessed but to be a blessing to others.

In Jesus' Name, Amen.

We are to bring our tithes and offerings before the Lord. Assuming you are faithful to tithe, what area of ministry do you, or will you, give your offerings to?

What are a few areas in which you would like to serve, giving your time and talents to the body of Christ?

DAY 7

Stronger Than

"Have I not commanded you? Be strong and of good courage; do not be afraid, nor be dismayed, for the LORD your God is with you wherever you go."
– Joshua 1:9, NKJV

Fear is one of our greatest enemies. When God gives us an assignment or allows a challenge, our default response is often panic. We feel overwhelmed and underqualified when we depend on our gifts, talents, and experiences. I do.

I know I fall short of what my Father deserves. Have you ever felt that uneasiness in your stomach? The dread of impending failure?

Today, be confident that God goes with you, as He did when Moses promoted Joshua as his successor. Now that's a tough act to follow.

Being distressed over the unknown is a natural human frailty. But declare right now that you are not the average, run-of-the-mill human. You have the God of the universe going ahead of you for direction surrounding you with protection. Do not let fear rob you of your faith and peace of mind. You are not alone.

No matter how challenging the circumstances may seem today or how hopeless the situation appears, the Lord is with you. You serve a God who is more than enough, causing you to be stronger than your struggles.

WALK IT OUT

Today, expect God to come through for you. When you face challenges, big or small, know that God will make a way.

You serve a God that is a waymaker, promise keeper, and able to part the seas to ensure that you get to the other side.

Heavenly Father,

I thank You for going ahead of me daily to make the crooked paths straight. I know I can walk in victory because You have promised me that wherever the soles of my feet tread, you have given me the land.

In Jesus' Name, Amen.

- ❧ Today, recall and record a time the Lord came through for you.

- ❧ Share this testimony with someone today.

DAY 8

Endless Mercy

"Let us then approach God's throne of grace with confidence, so that we may receive mercy and find grace to help us in our time of need."
– *Hebrews 4:16, NIV*

Here it is, straight -- our intentional sin and willful disobedience deserve God's judgment. Yeah, let's keep it real. That verse in Hebrews has gotten me through many times I knew I was failing God. Like every human, I come before God one hundred percent guilty. Oh, but that *mercy*. Ephesians 2:4-5 says, "But God, who is rich in mercy, because of His great love with which He loved us, even when we were dead in trespasses, made us alive together with Christ (by grace you have been saved)" (NKJV).

God is so loving towards us that He gave us an option for the death sentence we deserve. He gave us a way out if we accept Jesus Christ and the redemptive work of the cross. If you are His, you have access to God's great mercy and grace for salvation and for life. No matter the circumstances or how many times you miss the mark, God's forgiveness is there for you when you ask for it and turn away from your wrongs. I have heard it said — *Grace is when God gives us what we do not deserve; Mercy is when God does not give us what we do deserve.* Ask for mercy and walk in the freedom Jesus bought for you.

"AND FOR ALL THESE PEOPLE ALIKE, THE KEY TO HEALING TURNED OUT TO BE THE SAME. EACH HAD A HURT HE HAD TO FORGIVE."[9]

Corrie Ten Boom
The Hiding Place

WALK IT OUT

None of us deserve what we have; it's all been given to us by His grace and His mercy.

Today when you fall short, do not condemn yourself but ask God for mercy. He will gladly give it to you. God knows we are flawed, and sometimes we make bad decisions.

Accept God's mercy, and even though you are guilty, know He is quick to forgive.

Dear God,

I come to You as a sinner, undeserving of Your grace and mercy. I ask You to forgive me so that you may hear my request. I ask for Your favor today. Have mercy on me and fill me with Your grace. Thank You for Your faithfulness.

In Jesus' Name, Amen.

Using the description above, give an example of when God provided something you did not deserve (grace).

Now, give an example of when God protected you from a painful outcome you did deserve (mercy).

DAY 9

Your Decisions Determine Your Destiny

"But that isn't what you learned about Christ. Since
you have heard about Jesus and have learned the
truth that comes from him, throw off your old
sinful nature and your former way of life, which is
corrupted by lust and deception. Instead, let the
Spirit renew your thoughts and attitudes. Put on
your new nature, created to be like God—truly
righteous and holy."
— *Ephesians 4:20-24, NLT*

Your life is often a result of your choices. What you
choose is what you get. Whatever you have done in the
past, no matter what others have done to you, there
is a *going forward* with you behind the wheel. In this
moment, will you determine to set your life on a healthy

course? Be honest about what parts you have control over, and decide what helps you to your goal and what hinders you from reaching them. Search yourself and identify spots that need strengthening. Even if you're not responsible for the damage, you are accountable for the repairs . That's just the way it is for all of us — the ball's in your court.

Take responsibility. The moment you begin to hold yourself accountable for your actions and reactions, life will change for you. An active, positive response to trouble is a track to transformation. Any issue you encounter is a chance for change because God is always working things out for your good. When you stop making excuses, you will start seeing results.

***

EVEN IF YOU'RE NOT RESPONSIBLE FOR THE DAMAGE, YOU ARE ACCOUNTABLE FOR THE REPAIRS.

WALK IT OUT

Do you recognize the opportunity to change something around you? Maybe reroute your course or surround yourself with better influences?

Begin there.

Heavenly Father,

Help me accept the responsibility and the consequences of my actions. Help me to stop blaming others for the things that I have caused myself. Even when someone else was responsible for the pain, let me take responsibility for the healing. With your help, I know it's possible.

In Jesus' Name, Amen.

- Take a moment and identify one area of your life you can add to or strengthen.

- Identify an area that needs restriction or eviction (ie something that needs some limits or an area that needs to be completely eliminated.)

DAY 10

Consider the Source

"Every good and perfect gift is from above, coming down from the Father of the heavenly lights, who does not change like shifting shadows."
– *James 1:17, NIV*

God is our source. All the good in our lives comes from Him. It may go through your hard work; it may be spoken from your parent's mouth, or provided by a Christian brother or sister. But do not be confused -- the hand of God is where all good things originate, no matter what other hands they pass through.

You never know when God will get you over your situation through someone who gets under your skin.

So, keep your heart and mind open, accepting God's plan however He delivers it. Your trust and surrender will ensure the Creator gets all the credit.

Use wisdom because the enemy can also become a source. Just because it's a good idea doesn't make it a *God* idea. If the enemy is the source, it may start looking good but end badly.

Your employer might write your check, but the Lord gives you the ability to do the work. God also gives us the health we need to make wealth, the mind to be creative, the gifts and talents, the way we see things, our perspective – all God. We are not entitled to anything on our own merit, but through Christ, we have everything. Be thankful; don't take any good thing for granted, and in all things, consider your Source.

"BECAUSE GOD IS THE GIVER AND SOURCE OF OUR LIFE, HE HAS A LEGITIMATE CLAIM UPON OUR LIVES."[10]

Billy Graham

WALK IT OUT

Have you been praying about a major decision? Understand that your choices come with consequences. Putting it in writing can often bring clarity to your decision.

Heavenly Father,

I acknowledge that You are the source of every good thing in my life. Help me always to discern the difference between Your provision and the enemies' distractions.

Lead me and guide me and help me to stay in Your will.

In Jesus' Name, Amen.

Create a list of pros and cons about a decision you are considering.

DAY 11

Cut to the Chase

"There is a time for everything, and a season for
every activity under the heavens: a time to be born
and a time to die, a time to plant and a time to
uproot."
– Ecclesiastes 3:1-2, NIV

God wants to do something extraordinary in your life.
Are you ready to jump into action today? Maximize the
day in front of you – stop procrastinating. Time is an asset
you can never retrieve once it is gone. Your minutes and
hours, days and years are essential commodities. You
can begin creating your tomorrow today. Whatever is
in your future is decided in your present. With each day

and every decision, you are building the life unfolding down the road.

Take time to pray today so that you will be ready for tomorrow. You will plan and then prepare, perform, and produce. Get your praying on today, so tomorrow it starts paying off. Utilize your time wisely, and don't be derailed by details that distract you from your purpose.

When we manage our time correctly, we have more time to be used by God. Move into action and watch someone get set free. Someone is going to get saved; there will be healing because of the work you are doing through prayer and practical service. Do not hesitate to engage the enemy for your dreams or someone's needs. Take him on with the confidence that you are a child of God. What you do today affects tomorrow. God's going to bless you in such a great and mighty way.

WHATEVER IS IN YOUR FUTURE IS DECIDED IN YOUR PRESENT.

WALK IT OUT

Take time to schedule every activity in your day. The word schedule comes from the Latin for "a slip of paper."

Give every task a time to begin and a time to end. Soon you will see an increase in your effectiveness, productivity, and fruitfulness.

Heavenly Father,

Help me to be a good steward of my time. I know my time has limits on this earth, so help me to stay focused on Your will and the assignment You have for me.

Thank You for the wisdom and insight to stay on course.

In Jesus' Name, Amen.

In what ways have you made personal or professional progress recently in getting closer to your goals?

What obstacles do you face that may cause delays or setbacks in your schedule? What is one thing you can change to help remedy this issue?

DAY 12

Listen to Your Pain

"...Weeping may endure for a night, But joy comes in
the morning."
– Psalm 30:5, NKJV

Believe it or not, pain can be a good thing. In the body, "the nervous system triggers a sensation of pain to stop you from doing something that might cause a severe injury, and to let you know something is wrong"[11] so you can treat the source of the pain. Pain is discomfort created by disorder. It is the same in other aspects of our being – pain lets us know when we need to correct our focus, thinking, intentions, and motivations to get our behavior in order.

Ask God to help you pinpoint what type of pain you are dealing with. Are you mentally, emotionally sore from being stretched and strengthened? Or are the areas of tenderness and aching the result of unforgiveness or jealousy? Sin or selfishness?

Once you identify, you must rectify. Repair it. Target the correct enemy of your joy and peace and take your attitude shifts as a symptom of something deeper. Pain will have you wanting relief and willing to listen. Give your pain a purpose. Do not ignore the signals. Pain is a sign that something needs to change.

If your discomfort is the price of transitioning toward excellence, push through the pain and flush the toxins from your spiritual muscles. As with athletes, consume plenty of water – the living water of the Word.

PAIN LETS US KNOW
WHEN WE NEED
TO CORRECT OUR
FOCUS, TO GET OUR
BEHAVIOR IN ORDER.

WALK IT OUT

Much of the pain we experience can be self-inflicted. You're only as free as you are honest. Bring your pain to the Lord, and be specific.

Ask God to heal you. If you listen to your pain, it will speak to the areas that need to change.

Heavenly Father,

I know that You relate to my painful struggles. Jesus died a painful death so that He can relate to what I go through.

Today, I cast my cares on You because You care for me. I receive my healing, and I thank You that You will use the struggles of this life for my gain and Your glory.

In Jesus' Name, Amen.

❧ What type of pain are you dealing with presently? (Mental, emotional, financial, etc)

❧ Identify the root cause of your struggle. Ask the Holy Spirit to help you see it.

DAY 13

Mourning, Noon and Night

"God blesses those who mourn,
for they will be comforted."
– Matthew 5:4, NLT

During the pandemic, unfortunately, many of us heard of loved ones that passed away. COVID has given us another way to lose loved ones. Some families have had to bury one family member after another. One woman from my church lost seven relatives to the Coronavirus. Another is grieving his mother, his father, and now his sister – all within 30 days time. There are no words. So, we pray.

If you have lost loved ones, no matter the cause, you know it is a pain like no other. That first year or so of holidays without them, reaching for the phone only to remember they are gone — it is a shock to the system. So, we pray. We cry, we scream, we collapse, and we pray.

God is a God of comfort. He is a God of peace. He strengthens you when your knees buckle under the pressures of this world and losses that do not make sense. When my dad and brother passed away, there were people who sat with me. They were just there – loving, stabilizing friends when my heart was broken. If you know someone who is grieving, remember that words do not always offer relief. This is when you practice the ministry of *presence*. God offers a blessing of comfort to those who mourn. Be available – He may desire to comfort others through you.

"COMPASSION COSTS. IT IS EASY ENOUGH TO ARGUE, CRITICIZE, AND CONDEMN, BUT REDEMPTION IS COSTLY, AND COMFORT DRAWS FROM THE DEEP. BRAINS CAN ARGUE, BUT IT TAKES HEART TO COMFORT."[12]

Samuel Chadwick

WALK IT OUT

If you're grieving the loss of a loved one or know someone who is, take time to allow yourself to heal. Reach out to others who may be a blessing in your life with comfort and encouragement. There are bereavement support groups locally, and online that can help you navigate through the stormy waters of grief.

The Holy Spirit is your comforter; even when you feel lonely, know that you are never alone.

Lord,

I ask You to bring comfort. Give peace in the midst of pain, and hope for despair. Give me strength and help me to be a comfort to others who are in pain. When better days are hard to imagine, remind me of Your goodness. I am trusting in Your faithfulness to bring us out stronger on the other side.

In Jesus' Name, Amen.

❧ List a few family, friends, or co-workers who have experienced grief or illness in the past months and write a note or text of encouragement.

❧ Share these verses, or encourage yourself by writing them down and meditating on them. Isaiah 43:2; Isaiah 41:10; 2 Corinthians 1:3-5; Psalm 147:3; Psalm 73:26

DAY 14

Brave It Out

"Wait patiently for the Lord. Be brave and
courageous. Yes, wait patiently for the Lord."
– *Psalm 27:14, NLT*

We tend to want what we want when we want it – *now*.
Resisting the temptation to take matters into our own
hands builds our strength and fortifies our trust in God.
While you are waiting, God is working. James 1:4 says,
"But let patience have its perfect work, that you may be
perfect and complete, lacking nothing" (NKJV).

Patience is "the capacity to accept or tolerate delay,
trouble, or suffering without getting angry or upset."[13]

We can tolerate delay if we trust that God will work things out beautifully at the right time (Ecclesiastes 3:11). We persevere in trouble and suffering when we trust God to comfort us (2 Corinthians 1:3). Get the idea? Patience results from trusting our Father in Heaven, taking Him at His Word. With patience, we won't give up right before the breakthrough. We endure the opposing winds as we press on to the finish line. Our biggest challenge is impatience — wanting things now, quick, and in a hurry. We want drive-through timing from a gourmet God.

Job waited on the Lord and, eventually, he received twice as much as he had lost (Job 42:10). If you are in a challenging time (and who isn't), stick it out and trust the One you pledge your allegiance to. Believe this: trust and patience will play a powerful role in your next steps this week.

TO LOSE PATIENCE IS TO
LOSE THE BATTLE.

WALK IT OUT

When you're tempted to move ahead of God, remember that God's timing is always perfect. To lose patience is to lose the battle.

God's path isn't always a shortcut, but in the long run, it will get you to where you're supposed to be.

Heavenly Father,

When I desire immediate results, help me to wait on You. I know I can trust You to lead me down the right path.

Give me the patience for Your perfect will to be done in the right season.

In Jesus' Name, Amen.

❧ Is there something you are waiting on God for today? Write it below.

❧ There is a definition of *patience* in the second paragraph of today's devotional. Would you use those words to describe yourself? If not, how would you describe your demeanor when God makes you wait for what you want?

DAY 15

Safe and Secure

"The Lord will keep you from all harm — he will watch over your life; the Lord will watch over your coming and going both now and forevermore."
– *Psalm 121:7-8, NIV*

These are trying times we are living in. Life is stressful, and no one is exempt from workplace tensions, health issues, relationship struggles, parenting demands — or simply paying rent and car loans. Add to the everyday pressures the cultural climate of conflict exacerbated by the media, and we are ready to crumble. The enemy is on a 24/7 news cycle, piling on the worry. So, I ask you – who are you listening to?

Fear, uncertainty, and doubt are the enemy's greatest weapons. His desire is to confuse, conflict, and conquer our faith. Turn down the noise of this world, and turn up the volume of God's Spirit.

Your Creator and Protector says, "No weapon formed against you shall prosper" (Isaiah 54:17). Don't let fear hold you back from the fullness of what God has for your life. Keep stepping. Keep moving forward. Plead the blood of Jesus over your fear, and know that God is with you. The enemy will not succeed in pulling you out of the game. God has not given you a spirit of fear, but of power, love, and a sound mind (2 Timothy 1:7). If your mind is not sound (i.e. healthy, stable, reliable, wise, good), your thoughts are not from God. Refuse them. Reject them. Replace them with His promises. Walk in God's grace and God's goodness, and know that He is "a shield to those who put their trust in Him" (Proverbs 30:5).

DON'T LET FEAR HOLD
YOU BACK FROM THE
FULLNESS
OF WHAT GOD HAS
FOR YOUR LIFE.
KEEP STEPPING.

WALK IT OUT

Pray for God's protection over your life daily. Remember that God promises to keep you safe and secure under His wings of love.

Walk boldly in your calling, knowing that God's grace and mercy surround you.

Heavenly Father,

I thank You for surrounding me with Your angels. You have given me a shield of faith that quenches every fiery dart of the enemy. I cancel every work of the enemy today, and)though weapons will form, they will not prosper.

In Jesus' Name, Amen.

What weapon is the enemy using against your thoughts?

Knowing "no enemy formed against you will prosper," in what ways are you refusing and rejecting the fiery darts of his lies? What scriptures will you use to combat them?

DAY 16

You're as Free as You are Honest

"If we say that we have no sin, we deceive ourselves,
and the truth is not in us. If we confess our sins,
He is faithful and just to forgive us our sins and to
cleanse us from all unrighteousness."
– 1 John 1:8-9, NKJV

Everyone blows it. Not everyone shows it. Human beings do not enjoy revealing our weaknesses or mistakes. We want to be social media presentable, don't we? It is a trap, plain and simple. The adage, "You are only as sick as your secrets," is well known in addiction recovery. As humbling as it may be, no matter your struggle or sin, transparency is a vital part of the healing. Confess it, address it, and dispossess it. Really, who are we trying to fool? God sees and knows everything anyway.

Resist pride, deception, and blame-shifting. If you made a wrong choice, own it. Do not point it at someone else or hold your past responsible for your choices today. If you could have altered the trajectory of your life but did not, admit it. It is okay. Tomorrow is coming, and you can take yourself in a different direction. But only if you accept you were wrong. And admit it.

Confess your sin, and present yourself to your merciful God. Bring it before the Lord and say, *Father, forgive me, cleanse me, help me, strengthen me so that I do not continue to do these things.* Remember that Jesus is your advocate.

WALK IT OUT

Own your mistakes. Find an accountability partner that will be honest, loving, and truthful. Keeping yourself transparent eliminates the temptation to regress to the old you.

The Holy Spirit loves you and wants you to know that no matter how many times you have failed, He will never give up on you. So don't give up on yourself.

Merciful Lord,

Sometimes I make a mess of things. Show me if there is sin in my heart. Give me courage to face my defects and pride. Forgive me of my sins. Reveal to me when I am misguided and heal my deepest wounds. Thank You for Your mercy.

In Jesus' Name, Amen.

Today, make these verses your prayer and deep desire.

- Pray Psalm 139:23-24.

- Write Psalm 51:10-17.

DAY 17

Pray Strategically

"I am thankful to God, whom I have served with
a clear conscience as my ancestors did, when I
remember you in my prayers as I do constantly night
and day."
– *1 Timothy 1:3, NET*

Timothy was not always sure of himself; he could be hesitant and sometimes needed a push from his mentor. In his first recorded letter to his protégé, Paul assures him that even though he is not there in person, the apostle prays for him daily. Paul believed in the power of prayer; many are scattered throughout the thirteen New Testament books he authored. The apostle prayed for himself (2 Corinthians 12:7-9), and he requested people pray for him – actually, he required it (Ephesians 6:18-20). Paul prayed specifically. He prayed strategically, as is the habit of great intercessors like Job, Jeremiah, Esther – *you*.

We know we can talk to God anytime, anyplace. Still, I encourage you to find a dedicated space for doing real spiritual battle. Post the names of people who do not know the Lord and fight for their salvation through your faith-filled declarations. Categorize your prayer targets – healing, deliverance, salvation, finances, relationships, etc. And then "go into all the world" with your prayers (Mark 16:15). You may never be a missionary in a foreign land. Still, your intercession in Spirit-filled prayer will dispatch the angels across the world to minister to those who are ministering in every part of the world.

WALK IT OUT

Get a globe or a map; lay hands on it and speak salvation and peace into existence.

Do not doubt the power you have when you use your words of victory and confidence through the blood of Jesus and the power of the Holy Spirit.

Heavenly Father,

I know You hear my prayers and are faithful to answer them. Thank You for giving me the strategies and purpose to impact the world through prayer. I know that distance cannot limit the effectiveness of my prayers. Help me to be constantly aware that whoever I pray for, wherever they are, my prayers will reach them.

In Jesus' Name, Amen.

Pray strategically by categorizing your prayer targets below. Suggested categories are healing, deliverance, salvation, finances, relationships, etc.

DAY 18

The Battle Before the Blessing

"I trust in God, so why should I be afraid? What can mere mortals do to me?"
— *Psalm 56:11, NLT*

Warfare comes before the birth of a miracle. Look at the birth of our greatest miracle – Jesus. Around the time of His birth in Bethlehem, Herod killed all the baby boys from two years old and under. Jesus' parents took him down to Egypt until Herod died to keep their boy protected (Matthew 2). The enemy has been trying to deter your miracle and prevent your purpose since before *it* was old enough to walk. Believe that. You will have opposition on your way to your promised responsibility and reward.

When David showed up that day to give his brothers some lunch, they were fighting for Israel's good name. He overheard talk of the giant Philistine who came out every morning to taunt Saul and his army. No one could stand up to him. God gave little David just enough courage and confidence to man up. David's assurance was in the Lord. He trusted God to use whatever skills and weapons were available, i.e. five stones and a slingshot. Again, he was victorious with *a smooth stone and a slingshot*! The big guy goes down, and the little guy is raised up to be king. You see, the size of your enemy determines the size of your reward.

Conditions or other people may come against you; your weakness and desires might threaten to throw you off your game – when it happens, remind yourself of this: Spiritual warfare creates promotion. The barriers you face form opportunities for victory, validation, and value in your life and purpose.

THE SIZE OF YOUR ENEMY DETERMINES THE SIZE OF YOUR REWARD.

WALK IT OUT

When you pray for a miracle, realize that every advantage is surrounded by warfare. Use the authority that God has given you, *in Jesus' Name*, to destroy the works of the enemy. He is not an equal foe, so fight boldly, pray passionately, and expect to win.

With God on your side, the fight is fixed in your favor.

Father,

In the Name of Jesus, I destroy every work of the enemy against my life and in the lives of those I love. By Your great strength at work in me for battle, I decree that every power of the enemy that rises against me will be put down. Thank You, Holy Spirit, for guiding me to avoid every trick and every trap set up for me. Help me to walk in Your Way and live for Your glory.

In Jesus' Name, Amen.

When David faced Goliath, he recalled the many threats he had chased away with his slingshot while tending sheep. With that in mind, answer these questions:

- What Goliath do you face today?

- Recall and record a time in your past when God delivered you to victory. Let God's faithfulness strengthen your faith as you pick up your stone and slay your giant today.

DAY 19

Fulfill Your Mission

"For the dream comes through much effort and the
voice of a fool through many words."
— *Ecclesiastes 5:3, NASV*

To reach your goals and fulfill your mission, start where Moses did. You don't have to relax in a papyrus-reed basket to float toward success, but you must embrace God's vision. Moses received a picture from God for himself, his people, and for Israel. He did not get all the details when the Lord told him to "go, for I am sending you to Pharaoh. You must lead my people Israel out of Egypt" (Exodus 3:10, NLT). Moses knew nothing about how Jehovah would accomplish that monumental task, so he protested by reminding God of his *nothingness.* "Who am I to --? *But what if they --?*"

Sound familiar? With each argument of insecurity, God reminded Moses who his God was. The Lord gave Moses a preview of what He could do to prove His power and a vision of the miracles He would do through Moses. Even feeling incompetent, Moses took a step of faith and moved in the direction of God's appointment for him. When uncertain of your future because you are convinced of your frailty, remind your heart of God's faithfulness. If God's request seems ridiculously huge, and you become disillusioned and exhausted along the journey, return to the Father of your future for a pep talk. He will renew your vision and restore your strength. When you doubt you have the right stuff, remember – God knows what you are made of because He made you.

"GOD'S WORK DONE IN GOD'S WAY WILL NEVER LACK GOD'S SUPPLIES."

- HUDSON TAYLOR[14]

WALK IT OUT

You have an assignment. Fulfill your mission by embracing God's vision. Stay close to His Word, knowing He will reveal His plan through it.

Make God's Word a daily habit.

Don't say God doesn't speak if your Bible is closed.

Heavenly Father,

You have given me an assignment to fulfill. At times it seems too big and difficult to handle. I thank You, Lord, that it's my responsibility to be obedient, and it's Your responsibility to make it happen. I can put in the effort, knowing that You will do the heavy lifting.

In Jesus' Name, Amen.

When Moses felt ill-equipped for the task, he reminded God of his "nothingness." When an endeavor looks like too much for you, what excuses do you give yourself for not accepting the call, or giving up too soon?

God knows who you are because He made you. Who does He say you are? What does He say you're worth? Write down who you really are, according to God, and believe it.

DAY 20

Goddependant

"But he said to me, 'My grace is sufficient for you, for my power is made perfect in weakness.' Therefore I will boast all the more gladly about my weaknesses, so that Christ's power may rest on me."
— 2 Corinthians 12:9, NIV

Many people prefer to believe they are independent – especially those who have been hurt or let down by someone they thought they could trust. Can you relate to that? We trust a fallible human, and we become disappointed, either by the experience or our expectations. Once someone lets us down, we can react by relying on no one except number one. Thank God He loves us too much to keep us from Him. He will go so far as to allow an event we cannot handle alone to remind us we weren't created to – we need Him, and we need each other. It might feel uncomfortable, but there is no better place to be than total reliance on Christ. Difficulty is the seed that produces dependence, like in the case of Paul.

Whatever his "thorn in the flesh" refers to, our loving Father allowed it to remain in the apostle's life. Is your assurance in Jesus' love? God is consistent. Have you noticed? He sustains and strengthens you through the drizzle as well as the downpour. Overcoming constant conflict builds consistent confidence. Count on it. Stop drowning in worry; get out there and walk on the waves.

OVERCOMING
CONSTANT CONFLICT
BUILDS CONSISTENT
CONFIDENCE.

WALK IT OUT

Trust God in every situation, recognizing He always wants the best for you. Our faults and failures have proven that we can't do it on our own.

Depend on God because He is dependable. Put your faith in God because He is faithful. Rely on God because He is reliable.

Heavenly Father,

Help me to depend on You more and rely on me less. Help me to decrease so that You will increase in every area of my life.

I am grateful that when I call on You, You always show up. I put all my trust in You because You are faithful.

In Jesus' Name, Amen.

❧ Describe how someone has shown up for you recently.

❧ Identify the last time you needed help and asked for it. What happened?

DAY 21

On Principle

"Let integrity and uprightness preserve me, For I
wait for You."
– *Psalm 25:21, NKJV*

Integrity. In construction, the meaning of *integrity* is "durability." Ruling bodies like government, assemblies, or committees take an undivided stance of solidarity through "territorial integrity." Relating to electronic data, "integrity checking" determines internal consistency and lack of corruption. We know a *person* of integrity to be someone who holds ethical and moral principles — durable, united, consistent, honest. Being known as someone of character and integrity is hard won, especially if you have been known otherwise. One moment of weak moral commitment, and you can lose everything, including your reputation.

The Israelites successfully conquered the strongly fortified city of Jericho just to turn around and lose to the tiny town of Ai. How did Joshua suffer such a humiliating defeat? The mighty army was taken down because of one greedy foot soldier's integrity deficit and a weakness for silver, gold, and a nice robe. Defying God's command to take no spoils from their victory over the wicked city of Jericho (Joshua 6:19), Achan had taken a few choice items and hidden them in his tent until God revealed him to be the reason behind the upset at Ai. The consequences were devastating.

C.S. Lewis defines integrity as "doing the right thing, even when no one is watching." All of us, at one time or another, fall short when it comes to integrity. In times of weakness, tiredness, or unknown consequences, it's easy to compromise the truth. Don't allow your past failures to define your destiny. By receiving God's grace, mercy, and forgiveness, you will unlock the key to walking free of condemnation.

"INTEGRITY IS DOING THE RIGHT THING, EVEN WHEN NO ONE IS WATCHING."[15]

C.S. LEWIS

WALK IT OUT

"Let your 'yes' be 'yes,' and your 'no' be 'no'" (Matthew 5:37).

Don't make promises you can't keep. Let your word be your bond.

Take a moment and search your heart. If you need forgiveness, ask God to change your ways.

Heavenly Father,

Please forgive me for not keeping my promises. I want to be a person known for my integrity, honesty, and good character. Thank You for Your forgiveness, and help me to honor You through my actions.

In Jesus' Name, Amen.

In your own words, define *integrity*.

Go a Step Further: In Matthew 23, Jesus calls the religious leaders, "hypocrites." Read the passage and list the characteristics of the Pharisees who "do not practice what they teach."

DAY 22

Settle Up

"She said to herself, 'If I only touch his cloak,
I will be healed.'"
– *Matthew 9:21, NIV*

A famous maxim goes something like this: "The best predictor of future behavior is past behavior." That is a sad, hopeless forecast for a lot of people. Throughout the Bible and all across my life, I see a truth that should encourage you – Your future is decided by what you choose to believe. Like the woman with the issue of blood in Matthew 9, when you hope enough to reach for your best life, you can have it. You can walk in wholeness, think in completeness, and live in the fullness of God when you decide you want to be healed. Do not settle for a life that has let you down. It is time to settle UP. Look at this passage; take it in.

"Just then a woman who had been subject to bleeding for twelve years came up behind him and touched the edge of his cloak. She said to herself, 'If I only touch his cloak, I will be healed.' Jesus turned and saw her. 'Take heart, daughter,' he said, 'your faith has healed you.' And the woman was healed at that moment."
(Matthew 9:20-22, NIV)

Even after twelve years of suffering with an "unclean" illness, this faceless, nameless outcast of society believed for something better — a future that did not involve ridicule and rejection. The woman decided to change her future by reaching for the One who could release her to a different tomorrow. Make up your mind to be healed and whole and happy. Whatever chaos or calamity clutches onto you, cling to Jesus.

DO NOT SETTLE FOR A
LIFE THAT HAS LET YOU
DOWN.
SETTLE UP!

WALK IT OUT

Your comments have creative power. Learn to speak words of faith. What you say will determine your future.

Begin to think and expect good things to happen. Speak it over yourself, your family, your finances, and your health.

Heavenly Father,

I believe You always want the best for me. Change my heart so that my words will reflect my faith and trust in You. Help me to rest on Your love and boldly declare Your promises. You are the solid foundation on which I build my life.

In Jesus' Name, Amen.

❧ List an area or two in which you are believing for something better.

❧ Be your own cheering section: Look at your list and write a few statements of encouragement to yourself. Speak them out loud. It may feel awkward, but remember, a Word *spoken* formed the earth into existence.

DAY 23

Good God Almighty

"The Lord loves righteousness and justice; the earth
is full of his unfailing love."
– Psalm 33:5, NIV

Our God is good. The earth is full of the "goodness of the Lord" (Psalm 33:5, NKJV). God is a god of tenderness and displays His love through the outstretched arms of His Son on the cross. Christ took our place and paid our debt on Calvary. We are free and clear. Are you letting that truth catapult you into unshakeable joy? Are you filled with peace, assured of the covering the Father spreads over you?

God has arrested whatever the enemy intends for evil and ruin and molds it into something entirely for your advantage and advancement (Genesis 50:20). If you believe that, you will march through every frustration and catastrophe with boldness and an attitude of victory. Be confident that all things work together for your good (Romans 8:28). Your Designer and Developer wastes no material finishing the good work He has begun in you — mind, body, and soul (Philippians 1:6). Do you doubt your usefulness, thinking, *But, I have made too many mistakes. I'm too* _______ *and not enough* _______ when you recall your past?

We all have made mistakes, even with full knowledge that our actions were wrong. If that is your confession, you can still confidently proceed in your purpose because "God doesn't take back the gifts he has given or disown the people he has chosen" (Romans 11:29, CEV). Everything God does is good because He is good. Be assured of His kind-heartedness. Trust Him in every situation. Determine within yourself to shift your focus in the other direction because the Holy Spirit has a positive forecast for your future.

THE HOLY SPIRIT HAS A POSITIVE FORECAST FOR YOUR FUTURE!

WALK IT OUT

Stay focused on God's will for your life. Even the hard times are repurposed to form you into His image. Instead of asking, "Why did this happen," ask, "What can I learn from this?"

When circumstances don't make sense, that is when you have to trust that God is working everything out for your good.

Heavenly Father,

There are so many things that I don't understand and so many circumstances that make me ask "why." Lord, give me the faith and the strength to go forward even when there is no closure. Reveal Yourself to me in a greater way so my heart will be at peace.

In Jesus' Name, Amen.

🔥 List 5 ways God has shown His goodness in your life recently.

🔥 Name 5 ways you can show your faith in God.

DAY 24

Listen Carefully

"Let the wise listen to these proverbs and become even wiser. Let those with understanding receive guidance."
– *Proverbs 1:5, NIV*

We live in a day where we *overly* exercise our freedom to air our opinions. Many form their views through the influence of pop culture, celebrity viewpoints, and worldly philosophies. We can learn from everyone around us what to believe or not to believe. Somebody knows something you do not know. That information may be invaluable. You have to listen to receive it. We have two ears and one mouth, which means we should listen two times more than we speak. Something inside you may want attention. We all long to be heard. Restrain yourself.

Resist the temptation to express every thought. Just listen. So often, we listen to prepare our response. We need to be more attentive so we can gain understanding. Interrupting others while they're expressing themselves is tempting when you already have the answer you think they need. But if you listen a little longer, they will tell you what they need. Listen carefully to what God has to say in His Word. Gain understanding and wisdom, and you will find out that God is speaking. Are you willing to listen?

RESIST THE TEMPTATION
TO EXPRESS EVERY
THOUGHT.

WALK IT OUT

Fight the temptation to speak when you should be listening. It's not always natural because our attention span can be so short.

If you listen carefully and long enough, you will recognize what the other person is really communicating.

God wants to speak, but you have to be willing to listen.

Heavenly Father,

Help me to be a better listener and be more attentive to the way You are towards me. James 1:19 says to be quick to listen and slow to speak. I know that truth will help me gain more understanding and wisdom in my life. Thank You for always inclining Your ear towards me and answering my prayers.

In Jesus' Name, Amen.

If an unsaved person were to form an opinion about God based on your communication style, what would they come to believe about Him? (*He doesn't listen; He's judgmental*)

DAY 25

Wise Beyond Your Fears

"Getting wisdom is the wisest thing you can do! And whatever else you do, develop good judgment."
– Proverbs 4:7, NIV

Lessons in life will be repeated until they are learned. Wisdom is the ability to discern differences in people, environments, opportunities, and moments. Wisdom is the correct application of knowledge.[16] It is using sound judgment based on what you know. Solomon said that wisdom is the key that unlocks life's house of treasure (Proverbs 3:19-20). Attaining wisdom requires effort, time, and persistence. Ask yourself, *Am I making the right decision? Is there a lesson that I can learn from a decision that I made yesterday?* I want to encourage you today to seek the Lord first in every decision you make.

With the Holy Spirit's counsel at every turn, there is no reason to fear.

"But seek first the kingdom of God and His righteousness, and all these things shall be added to you."
(Matthew 6:33, NKJV)

Ralph Waldo Emerson said, "Knowledge is the antidote to fear."[17] The more we understand, the less uncertainty we feel; walking in wisdom is living confidently. And wisdom comes from a genuine, experiential understanding and respect of who the Almighty God is. As you grow in the Lord, your wisdom will grow as well. The Word of God is filled with great direction, and the Bible refers to Jesus as our Great Counselor. When we put our trust in the Lord, we do not have to depend on our own understanding.

"All Scripture is inspired by God and is useful to teach us what is true and to make us realize what is wrong in our lives. It corrects us when we are wrong and teaches us to do what is right." (2 Timothy 3:16-17, NLT)

When we put our trust in God and seek His ways and wisdom, we can worry less and be confident in Him.

LESSONS IN LIFE WILL BE REPEATED UNTIL THEY ARE LEARNED.

WALK IT OUT

Learning is the opportunity to expand your thinking. Every day you must be intentional about learning new things and increasing your understanding. Challenge yourself to read a book, learn to do a new task, or take a course.

Wisdom will lead you to the right source of information found in God's Word.

Heavenly Father,

Help me open my heart and mind to learn new things and better myself every day. Give me the wisdom to understand and utilize this information in a way that will glorify You. You said You would give me wisdom if I asked for it. So today, I ask for wisdom, understanding, and divine insight to complete the assignment You've given me.

In Jesus' Name, Amen.

Think of a wrong or misguided choice you've made. What is the lesson you can draw from that mistake?

DAY 26

Take Tiny Steps

"Do not despise these small beginnings, for the LORD rejoices to see the work begin, to see the plumb line in Zerubbabel's hand. (The seven lamps represent the eyes of the LORD that search all around the world.)"
– *Zachariah 4:10, NIV*

Stay in motion. Keep moving, even if it's a little at a time. Break down your goals into small steps and celebrate the small wins on the way. Champions are willing to move forward an inch at a time because progress creates joy. Two things are more important than money: your energy and time. Identify time-wasters that consume your energy, then limit their access to you. The enemy will always send people your way to distract, delay, and disrupt your progress. Use wisdom to stop them from wasting your time. Every day is important because small steps matter. How do you eat an elephant? You guessed it: *one bite at a time*. A race is performed one stride at a time, but one step can make all the difference between a win and a loss. Even just turning your head for a moment could be enough distraction to cause you to lose. My mother-in-law, Carmen Torres, would often quote from Paul's letter to the Philippians where the apostle Paul challenged himself and all Christians to keep moving forward in the Christian walk of faith:[18]

"Brethren, I do not count myself to have apprehended; but one thing I do, forgetting those things which are behind and reaching forward to those things which are ahead, I press toward the goal for the prize of the upward call of God in Christ Jesus" (Philippians 3:13–14, NKJV).

Stay focused on what is ahead of you. Keep your eyes on the prize. Don't compare yourself to others. Find your pace of grace, and you will win the race that God has assigned you to win.

WALK IT OUT

Stay focused on the assignment God has for you. Your big dreams are attainable, but it takes consistency, commitment, and concentration.

Keep moving one step at a time every day. It's just a matter of time before you reach the prize.

Heavenly Father,

When I get tired on my journey, give me the strength to continue day by day, one step at a time. When I get discouraged, remind me that You will reward my diligent effort. Thank You, Lord, for entrusting and equipping me to run this race and win.

In Jesus' Name, Amen.

❧ Name your "elephant." Write down a daunting, or difficult task you are facing.

❧ Identify the "small bites" required to complete this responsibility.

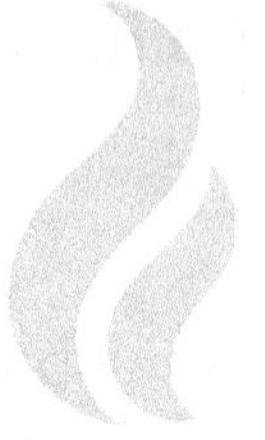

DAY 27

Remember Your Past

"He told them, "Go into the middle of the Jordan,
in front of the Ark of the LORD your God. Each of
you must pick up one stone and carry it out on your
shoulder—twelve stones in all, one for each of the
twelve tribes of Israel. We will use these stones to
build a memorial. In the future your children will ask
you, 'What do these stones mean?' Then you can tell
them, 'They remind us that the Jordan River stopped
flowing when the Ark of the LORD's Covenant went
across.' These stones will stand as a memorial among
the people of Israel forever."
– Zachariah 4:10, NIV

Recalling your past successes will help you to overcome
present obstacles. Think about your past battles and
struggles. Do you recall how God delivered you? David
remembered and replayed his victories over the bear

and the lion before he ran toward Goliath (1 Samuel 17:37). Those memories reinforced and renewed David's faith as he faced this great giant. If God did it before, He can do it again. As you face your giants today, whatever that may represent, remember that you have been in this position before, and God carried you through. Remember the victories, talk about them. Your Deliverer is prepared to show up again and give you the victory. Satan is the only one you will irritate.

"NOTHING PARALYZES OUR LIVES LIKE THE ATTITUDE THAT THINGS CAN NEVER CHANGE. WE NEED TO REMIND OURSELVES THAT GOD CAN CHANGE THINGS. OUTLOOK DETERMINES OUTCOME. IF WE SEE ONLY THE PROBLEMS, WE WILL BE DEFEATED; BUT IF WE SEE THE POSSIBILITIES IN THE PROBLEMS, WE CAN HAVE VICTORY."

Warren Wiersbe

WALK IT OUT

Don't forget how God got you through past situations that made you feel hopeless. Keep a journal and document those glorious events.

God loves you and will always defend you no matter how big the enemy may seem.

Don't be discouraged.

God is bigger.

Heavenly Father,

I thank You because You are with me no matter what I face today. So many times in the past when I felt hopeless and helpless, You came to my rescue and saved the day. I can always count on You. I am grateful that I don't fight alone, that the battle is Yours, but the victory is mine. Thank You, Father.

In Jesus' Name, Amen.

Recall how God has delivered you in the past and record it below.

In what way do you need Him to deliver you today? Ask Him now.

DAY 28

Linger in God's Presence

"You will show me the path of life: in your presence
is fulness of joy; at your right hand are pleasures for
evermore."
— *Psalm 16:11, NKJV*

The people present in your life make the most significant impact on where you're going. I remember my high school gym teacher, Mr. Dieppa. He took me under his wing and invited me to play basketball at the Fieldhouse in Chicago's Humboldt Park. I loved being in his presence because he made me feel good about myself. I was the youngest kid playing, but Mr. Dieppa helped me with my shot. When the opposing team saw how little I was, they underestimated my skill and left me open. I was hitting those shots because Mr. Dieppa believed in me and poured his experience into me. It gave me the confidence to go up against the bigger, older guys.

Linger long enough in His presence to understand what is required. Something happens in the presence of God that does not happen anywhere else. God's presence not only lifts burdens from our hearts but also reframes our opinion of our circumstances.

Your views will change in His presence. Your perceptions are corrected in His presence. Your faith becomes focused in His presence. In God's presence, Isaiah could see himself as he really was (Isaiah 6:5).

Allow God to reveal your true condition and humbly accept the Lord's revisions. God's presence also comes wrapped in the power to change and carry out your assignment. Those who surround you influence what you become.

THOSE WHO SURROUND
YOU INFLUENCE WHAT
YOU BECOME.

WALK IT OUT

When everyone else is in a hurry to get out of church, linger in God's presence and reflect on the moment.

Review and plan to apply the sermon you just heard.

Take time to pray and ask God to help you implement your strategy for the week.

Heavenly Father,

In Jesus' Name, thank You for Your presence in my life. Fill me afresh and anew with Your Holy Spirit. Help me to pursue my change by applying Your Word to my life. Thank You for making me the person You desire for me to be.

In Jesus' Name, Amen.

❧ Name someone who has played a pivotal role in your development as a person. How is your life better because of that person.

❧ Ask God to show you who you can impact through mentorship.

DAY 29

Fight by Fasting

"So we fasted and earnestly prayed that our God would take care of us, and he heard our prayer."
– Ezra 8:23, NIV

When I came to faith in Christ, I was a hot mess. I had deeply rooted issues, a dysfunctional mindset, chronic depression, and a host of other problems. One Sunday, my pastor taught on fasting, and I decided to try it. *What did I have to lose? Maybe a few pounds?*

Wow! It changed my life! God started to set me free from everything I was struggling with. It was amazing. Since that impactful experience, I fast on a weekly basis.

Fasting is an act that Christians have practiced since Biblical times. It's a faith-based discipline that helps us grow closer to God. Do you desire to be closer to God? Fasting is a sacrificial act demonstrating that your spiritual hunger for God is greater than your physical hunger for food.

Even our Savior, Jesus Christ, our most outstanding spiritual example, instructed us to fast. Mark 9:29 says, "So He said to them, 'This kind can come out by nothing but prayer and fasting'" (NKJV).

The disciples were trying to cast out a demon tormenting a young man. They prayed for quite a while to no avail. Jesus showed up and immediately freed the boy from his satanic bondage. He revealed to His disciples that fasting and praying was the key to their power!

You may have never fasted before; that's okay. Try it. I guarantee it will transform your life! When you deny your flesh, expect your spirit man to grow stronger and your prayer life more effective! Commit today to deny yourself something you like for a deeper connection to the God you love.

COMMIT TODAY
TO DENY YOURSELF
SOMETHING YOU LIKE
FOR A DEEPER CONNECTION TO
THE GOD YOU LOVE.

WALK IT OUT

Pick a day, skip breakfast, read your Bible, and pray.

Make God's Word and prayer your meal replacement. (I usually fast breakfast and lunch before I go to church on Wednesday.)

Holy God,

I pray for the desire and discipline to fast. I need certain areas in my life to change. I keep struggling, but I'm ready to be free. Holy Spirit, teach me to walk in God's ways so I can be delivered from all my sin, worries, fear, confusion, and bitterness.

Thank You, Lord. I receive my freedom today!

In Jesus' Name, Amen.

⸎ List a few areas where you can "deny your flesh" to spend time with God.

⸎ Prayerfully consider your commitment and describe your plan below. Be specific. (type of fast, duration, frequency, etc.)

DAY 30

Finish What You Start

"And all nations will hate you because you are my followers. But everyone who endures to the end will be saved."
– *Mathew 10:22, NIV*

God has given every one of us a mission to complete. Stay on course. Many tasks have an unpleasant side, but we must stay focused on the end result. Just know that with every blessing comes a burden. And, in many cases, a battle! Keep moving forward. Don't allow the challenge to hinder your progress. If God brings you to it, He'll see you through it. In reference to reaching his goal, Paul wrote, "Brothers and sisters, I do not consider myself yet to have taken hold of it. But one thing I do:

Forgetting what is behind and straining toward what is ahead, I press on —" (Philippians 3:13, NIV).

Unfortunately, we have an enemy that is always trying to create distractions to keep us from finishing our race. He knows our weaknesses and does all that he can to exploit them. He is an expert at laying down snares to interfere with God's plan and set us up for defeat. King David's prayer is recorded in Psalm 31:4: "Keep me free from the trap that is set for me, for you are my refuge." (NIV)

Just know that everything God does is opposed by warfare. The good news is that you are not alone. He will guide you around the landmines in the road! He knows what's ahead, and He'll either provide a detour to avoid the conflict or give you the wisdom to diffuse every bomb. Finish what you start, and God will increase your capacity for more!

FINISH WHAT YOU START,
AND GOD WILL INCREASE
YOUR CAPACITY
FOR MORE!

WALK IT OUT

Don't procrastinate. Stop putting off what you know should be done. Start tying up all your loose ends so you can declutter your mind.

Use your time wisely.

Don't commit to what you can't complete, but complete what you've committed to.

Father God,

Teach me to use my time wisely. Help me finish what I start to be more like You. You are "the author and the finisher of my faith," so I rely on Your Spirit to keep me focused until the job is complete.

In Jesus' Name, Amen.

❧ What is your "mission?"

❧ What does the phrase, "If God brings you to it, He'll see you through it," mean to you?

DAY 31

Seek God's Wisdom

"By wisdom a house is built, and through understanding it is established; through knowledge its rooms are filled with rare and beautiful treasures."
– Proverbs 24:3-4, NLT

Making decisions is something we do daily. Some are small: *What do I wear? What's for dinner?* Other choices can have a major impact on our lives. Avoid making a permanent decision on a temporary emotion. The accomplishments the Lord has for our future depend on it.

Wisdom will always be a more valuable guide than our emotions. Too often, we build our thoughts on the foundation of feelings. Our perception of our circumstances also dictates them. If we make our choices at times when our emotions are erratic, we take the risk of making some big mistakes. Rick Warren said, "Humility is not denying your strengths, rather, it is being honest about your weaknesses."[19]

Don't be too proud to ask for help. Many people fail because their pride keeps them from asking for assistance, and instead, they have to learn the hard way from painful experiences.

 "When pride comes, then comes shame; But with the humble is wisdom." (Proverbs 11:2, NKJV)

It's humbling to admit we don't have all the answers, but it's a *God* idea to get direction from godly men and women willing to mentor you. Surround yourself with people who love you, can pray for you, and give you sound, godly advice.

AVOID MAKING A PERMANENT DECISION ON A TEMPORARY EMOTION.

WALK IT OUT

Don't make decisions when you're in your feelings. Emotional choices usually lead to disasters.

Pray daily for God's wisdom, and He'll give it to you.

Be careful with the people you associate with. Surround yourself with people who are where you want to be.

Thank You, Lord, for the wisdom that is available to me daily. Remind me to remain humble and know I do not have all the answers —but You do. Lead me throughout my days that every decision I make will glorify You.

Bring people into my path who can become a resource and a blessing to my life — people full of wisdom and love.

In Jesus' Name, Amen.

What is the enemy of wisdom, according to Proverbs 11:2?

One Step Further: Read Proverbs 3 and Proverbs 19:21. What do these passages tell us is the secret to making consistently wise, godly choices?

DAY 32

Power to Endure

"But those who trust in the LORD will find new strength. They will soar high on wings like eagles. They will run and not grow weary. They will walk and not faint."
– *Isaiah 40:31, NLT*

Waiting is one of the most challenging positions for many of us. Waiting in line at the grocery store is tough. Sitting in a long line of cars at the bank is torture. Bumper-to-bumper traffic is excruciating. It takes endurance to remain patient.

The reason waiting is so tricky is we're always in a rush. We want things *now*! We want microwave potatoes, instant oatmeal, drive-thru, and fast-food prayer responses from God.

In the Bible, James reminds us to "let patience have its perfect work, that you may be perfect and complete, lacking nothing" (James 1:4).

Planting a seed of patience and watering it with endurance will always yield a good harvest. Building your determination to wait on God, though it may be difficult, is necessary to move at God's pace. At times, to experience God's best, we must endure seasons of waiting.

Getting ahead of God and taking things into your own hands, can birth something you may regret later. Abraham and Sarah became impatient, and instead of having an Isaac, they birthed an Ishmael. Even today, the tribe of Ishmael (Muslims) are mortal enemies of Israel. Endurance comes from knowing God, trusting God, and knowing that He'll always have your best interest in mind!

"ENDURANCE IS PATIENCE CONCENTRATED."

Thomas Carlyle

WALK IT OUT

Stay in it to win. Determine in your heart not to quit, no matter how long it takes to see God's promise come to life. Walking by faith and not by sight isn't always easy, but the outcome will always be right.

Enduring hardship, and overcoming persistent resistance is not designed to hurt you but to build strong muscle in the arena of life.

Dear Lord,

I don't always see what You are doing, but I know You're always working. Enable me to hang in there when all of me wants to give up. I know that Your delay is not necessarily Your denial but an opportunity to trust and endure until I receive Your best.

In Jesus' Name, Amen.

 Hebrews 11:6 says, "Without faith, it is impossible to please him [God]." What would you say is the relationship between patience and faith?

 One Step Further: Read James 1:2-4. Knowing that Christ was the only flawless person, what does James mean by "you may be perfect?"

DAY 33

You Represent Christ

So we are Christ's ambassadors; God is making his appeal through us. We speak for Christ when we plead, "Come back to God!"
– 2 Corinthians 5:20, NLT

Everywhere we go, people are watching, listening, and looking. People are people *watchers*. They will notice what you wear, who you're with, where you go, and what you listen to. Whether we like it or not, we are constantly leading others. We can be annoyed by this phenomenon or appreciate the opportunity to draw others to Christ. It was clear to Him that people would follow and imitate Him. We are given a daily opportunity as Christ's followers to be an example of the love, grace, mercy, and healing Christ has shown to us, whether we do so through words or actions. As Christ's ambassadors, we appeal to others on His behalf, pleading, "Come back to God" (1 Corinthians 5:20). How others perceive Christianity will always be impacted by what we say and do. We can forget these principles when we are busy, upset, or challenged by others. As we seek the Lord's help, let's ask ourselves, *Am I attracting others to Christ or influencing them away from Christ?* It is wonderful to know that we can ask the Lord to help us be a light that draws people to Jesus' healing and powerful presence.

WALK IT OUT

Today, look for opportunities to be a witness for Jesus. Embrace the guidance of the Holy Spirit and allow Him to connect you with people who need to meet such a powerful and almighty Savior.

Do not be ashamed of the gospel. Be prepared to be its ambassador! Cause everything about you to reveal what God has done for you.

Heavenly Father,

Thank You so much for changing my life. The peace and power that have transformed me into who I am today are beyond my comprehension. I desire to share this transforming joy that has changed my life. Use me for Your glory as I submit myself to Your purpose in my life.

In Jesus' Name, Amen.

❧ Today's devotional encourages us to ask ourselves, "*Am I attracting others to Christ or influencing them away from Christ?*" Courageously ask the Holy Spirit to reveal behaviors or attitudes you exhibit that may contradict Jesus.

❧ Describe a recent interaction in which someone could clearly see the love of Jesus through your actions.

DAY 34

Be Wise and Rise

"The way of a fool is right in his own eyes, But he
who heeds counsel is wise."
— *Proverbs 12:15, NKJV*

When God is the foundation of your life, asking for His wisdom helps you build a strong house filled with His blessings and favor. He wants us to be "healthy, wealthy, and wise!"[20] When we use wisdom to make good choices, we'll need fewer miracles to fix the bad ones. God's wisdom reveals what to do and when to do it.

In all reality, we've all made our share of poor choices. It's easy to get ahead of God and ask Him to follow *us*. Regrettably, when we do that, our limited vision can't reveal all the barriers and obstacles down the road. Then, when we hit a brick wall, we wonder why.

The good news is that no matter what mess we get into, God never holds it against us or criticizes us; He'll always step in and make things right (Psalm 103:10-18). We may have to deal with some consequences of our actions, but God promises to always turn it around for our good, making us stronger than before (1 Peter 5:10). All we have to do is ask.

"If any of you lacks wisdom, let him ask of God, who gives to all liberally and without reproach, and it will be given to him." (James 1:5, NKJV)

God encourages us to pray for His wisdom so that we can become like a magnet attracting all the good things He has for us. Being wise will help us rise above the circumstances and stay below the radar of the enemy's attacks.

"JUST BECAUSE
SOMETHING IS COMMON
SENSE DOESN'T MEAN IT'S
COMMON PRACTICE."
Will Rogers

WALK IT OUT

Commit to reading a chapter of Proverbs every day for a month. There are 31 chapters, so that coincides perfectly. Read them out loud so the words resonate in your heart and create the faith needed to do what you learn.

Heavenly Father,

In Jesus' name, give me the wisdom I need to stay on Your path with my choices. Thank You for not holding my mistakes against me so I can live without condemnation. Send the right people into my life so that I can get wise counsel and allow the Holy Spirit to lead me. Amen!

In Jesus' Name, Amen.

❧ God told Solomon he would give him anything he wanted. What did Solomon choose?

❧ What would you choose and why?

DAY 35

Walk Purely

"Blessed are the pure in heart, For they shall
see God."
— *Matthew 5:8, NKJV*

You are the offspring of a Holy God. Naturally, you will have an insatiable appetite for living a holy and pure life because you are created in Your Father's image. Nevertheless, sin happens in all of us. We live in a fleshly earth suit with worldly desires and an appetite to satisfy its own needs. Thank God, He is never out of reach.

"*Behold, the Lord's hand is not shortened, that it cannot save; neither His ear heavy, that it cannot hear: But your iniquities have separated between you and your God, and your sins have hid His face from you, that He will not hear.*" (Isaiah 59:1, KJV)

Don't try to cover your mistakes or weaknesses; whatever it is, bring it to God. Unconfessed sin separates you from God and harms your relationship with Him. Disobedience not only hurts you, but it hurts those around you. Repentance will open the door to the next season of your life.

Walk in obedience. Ask God to forgive you and to give you the strength not to go back down that road. Turn away from your sins and run into the forgiving arms of Jesus. You were made pure by His forgiveness, and you will stay pure by your obedience.

YOU ARE THE OFFSPRING
OF A HOLY GOD.

WALK IT OUT

Take time to take inventory of your life today. Look for areas you haven't surrendered to the Lord and places in your behavior or character where you fall short. Write them down.

Confess your sin, turn away from it, and pray that the Lord will keep you on His path.

Lord Jesus, forgive me.

I confess my sin to You. I know You died on the cross for my sins and You've taken my punishment upon Yourself. I repent from my sin and surrender my life to You. Create in me a pure heart. Thank You that my name is written in Your Book of Life.

In Jesus' Name, Amen.

- What areas do you hesitate to surrender?

- What is the best / worst you imagine happening if you turn away from these thoughts or behaviors?

- What is the best / worst that could happen if you don't surrender?

DAY 36

God's Plan Includes People

"Ask, and it shall be given you; seek, and ye shall find; knock, and it shall be opened unto you."
— *Matthew 7:7, KJV*

God never intended for us to succeed alone. Often, what we need is found in someone else. Are you willing to ask for help? The evidence of your desire and commitment to succeed is proven in your willingness to reach out for help when you need it. None of us has all the gifts necessary to accomplish the great plan God has for us.

When God desires to do mighty things *through* us, He will bring others *to* us to help fulfill the vision.

I love basketball, and being from Chicago, I'm a huge Bulls fan. Michael Jordan was a great player and received many individual awards, but he didn't start winning championships until the right team surrounded him. Even Jesus chose twelve disciples to continue His vision.

The Lord designed us to live in community. Reaching out to others for assistance is a sign of humility and wisdom. Many of God's promises are fulfilled when *two or more* "agree" (Matthew 18:19), or "are gathered" in His name (Matthew 18:20), or come together in love to persuade a fallen believer to turn back to God (Matthew 18:15-16). There is strength in unity, God shows up, and miracles happen. We are good alone, but we are much better together.

ARE YOU WILLING TO ASK
FOR HELP?

WALK IT OUT

Join a Bible-believing church and serve in a ministry. Become part of a team that has the same passion for helping others.

The key to your calling is the people group you are naturally and passionately drawn to help. And when you need assistance, resist your pride and ask for it.

Heavenly Father,

Help me put aside my pride and ask for help when needed. Independence is not a strength when it leads to isolation, so keep me connected to others. You died for me, and I pray that I can also sacrifice my time, talents, and treasure for others to know You. Use me to Your glory.

In Jesus' Name, Amen.

- What are your innate interests and talents? In what areas do you have experience?

- What group of people do you find yourself most concerned about?

- Look at your answers and identify an area in your church or community where you can serve with your skills and strengths. Now, connect with someone and get the ball rolling!

DAY 37

Focus by Fasting

"But you, when you fast, anoint your head and wash
your face,"
— Matthew 6:17, NKJV

Fasting will empower you to stay focused on what God is doing in your life. Notice that Jesus said, *when* you fast...not *if* you fast! Christ is implying that fasting is supposed to be a regular part of our lives. This powerful discipline makes our prayer life turbocharged and much more focused.

I remember coming to a crossroads in my life where I had to make a serious decision. I had an amazing job offer, but it would limit my time in church. After a time of fasting and prayer, God gave me peace, and I knew I had to turn it down. It was difficult because I was unemployed at the time. But God is faithful. The following week I received a job offer, not as much money, but I would be able to continue my involvement in ministry.

"For what will it profit a man if he gains the whole world, and loses his own soul? Or what will a man give in exchange for his soul?" (Mark 8:36–37, NKJV)

Fasting will focus you on God's will, not your own. At the end of the day, God may take you down a rocky road, but the bumpy conditions along the way help you appreciate the destination even more.

FASTING WILL FOCUS YOU ON GOD'S WILL, NOT YOUR OWN.

WALK IT OUT

Get Jentzen Franklin's book, *Fasting: Opening the Door to a Deeper, More Intimate, More Powerful Relationship with God.*

Read and learn how fasting enhances your life and creates a more intimate and powerful relationship with God.

My Lord and Savior,

I need Your will to be done in all the decisions and choices I make. As I fast today, allow me to clearly hear the direction I should go, and have the faith to step out on Your Word. Thank You for Your guidance.

In Jesus' Name, Amen.

❧ What are a few ways God may reveal or confirm His will to us?

❧ Look at your list. Which source is the one in which all others must agree in order to truly be from God?

❧ When facing a huge decision or challenge, name a few distractions you can eliminate to hear from the Holy Spirit better.

DAY 38

Cleaning Up Hand-Me-Down Messes

"Don't copy the behavior and customs of this world, but let God transform you into a new person by changing the way you think. Then you will learn to know God's will for you, which is good and pleasing and perfect."

"Actions have consequences." We know this on a scientific level and a spiritual level. Many of us have suffered or celebrated as a result of our choices. It's one thing to take on the task of putting out our self-started fires, but suffering the effects of someone else's mischief, mayhem, and misdeeds is a messy other thing altogether — especially if that someone is family.

For two generations, King Josiah had no godly examples in his life. His father and grandfather, Manasseh, were both corrupt kings. 2 Kings 21 details Granddad's wickedness -- raising altars and wooden images to Baal in the house of the Lord, sacrificing his own son in fire, and practicing witchcraft. But the Spirit of God planned a different path for Josiah. Instead of following in his family's idolatrous footsteps, the Lord made King Josiah responsible for cleaning up their mess and turning Judah back to God's Word (2 Kings 22:8-13).

Have you ever been tempted to excuse your behavior and choices by blaming the cards you were dealt? Do you get stuck in a loop, feeling destined to repeat the same unhealthy, ungodly lifestyle you grew up around? The "sins of the fathers" can become a crutch, a justification, or a set-up for failure. Or you can identify the problems, see the consequences as a warning of worse to come, and accept that not being responsible for the chaos does not mean you are not accountable for the clean-up.

"IN GOD'S WORLD, MANY FAILED FATHERS HAVE HAD RIGHTEOUS AND USEFUL SONS."[21]

John Piper

WALK IT OUT

I encourage you to begin noticing areas where you let yourself off the hook because *it's not my responsibility* or *I didn't cause the problem.*

"Responsibility is task-focused. It relates to a person's role in completing a certain task. Accountability is results-focused. It relates to how a person reacts or owns the results of their task."[22]

Savior,

Thank You that by Your stripes I am healed, and now I ask You to look over my family and heal our brokenness. Help each of us to take responsibility to right the wrongs we have caused and move forward in healing. Help me to humble myself and hold myself accountable for my choices.

In Jesus' Name, Amen.

What do you consider to be two major turning points in your life?

DAY 39

Test It

"Do not conform to the pattern of this world, but be transformed by the renewing of your mind. Then you will be able to test and approve what God's will is—his good, pleasing and perfect will."
— Romans 12:2, NIV

The world is filled with imitations. We are surrounded by hidden agendas, and deception that holds just enough *real* to be convincing. Author David Stevens said, "A lie is a lie even if everyone believes it. The truth is the truth even if nobody believes it." With social media influencing our conclusions, many people are persuaded by quantity of information, not quality. We repeat and repost and regurgitate this opinion, that report, and these statistics without doing our due diligence to be sure what we are sharing is true —perhaps because someone we admire posted the information. Or because the opinion matches the one we prefer to believe. I have seen good people copy satirical posts, commenting as though the info was true. Why? Because they didn't take the time to notice the source or investigate the information before spreading it. Be very careful what you believe and how you go about deciding what is true and what is false. If it doesn't settle in your spirit, then be very cautious going forward. Do not be swayed by opinions that do not come from God. God does open doors, but so does the enemy. The enemy will try to trap you through unhealthy desires and give you excuses to deceive yourself into compromising. God does not want us to be super critical, but neither does His Spirit abandon us to be gullible and naïve. Be confident in what you believe by being diligent in why you believe it.

BE CONFIDENT IN WHAT YOU
BELIEVE BY BEING DILIGENT
IN WHY YOU BELIEVE IT.

WALK IT OUT

God cannot contradict His character.

If you have come to know Him through time with Him in prayer, worship, and the Word, you will discern more readily what is and is not of Him.

Above all else, test all things against the Sovereign Word of God.

Father God,

Thank You that You are the same today as You were yesterday, and will be tomorrow. Help me to hear Your Holy Spirit, renewing my mind through the washing of the Word so that I can be confident in what is of You and what is not. Give me discernment to not only make wise choices, but in the course of it all to know I can trust Your guiding hand.

In Jesus' Name, Amen.

What are 2 or 3 major truths upon which you have based your decision-making?

DAY 40

In With the New

"So you must live as God's obedient children. Don't slip back into your old ways of living to satisfy your own desires. You didn't know any better then."
— 1 Peter 1:14, NLT

"Stop shrinking to fit places you've outgrown!"[23] Sounds funny, but how often do we find ourselves trying to fit into a situation where we no longer belong? The beautiful thing about coming to faith in Christ is we are given the opportunity for rebirth. It's a chance to begin again — a fresh start. When we come to Christ, The Lord has a whole new life He wants us to embrace. No more living the way we used to be. Depressed, broken, unhappy, or unfulfilled. Many times we can become frustrated because the decisions we have made in the past has driven us in the circles, the cul-de-sac of frustrations and dead end roads that have no way out. The greatest gift of coming to know Jesus as your personal Savior is we can become new in Christ. His plan for our lives is much better than anything we desire. Please make no mistake about it. When you surrender your heart to Jesus, He makes you brand new. God wants to give you a new life; as you grow in Him, you will become more like Him. So it's out with the old self and in with the new you.

When I gave my heart to Christ, I knew it would be very easy to slip back into my old ways, as the Apostle Peter says. That is why I joined my local church, connected in a small bible study, and allowed the Lord to reshape and repurpose my life. It worked! I became a new person filled with joy and purpose. You can, too. You don't have to fall into the temptation of reverting to your old sinful life. You can't win the world by conforming to it! Stand out and be counted. You represent God now in everything you say and do.

YOU CAN'T WIN THE WORLD BY CONFORMING TO IT!

WALK IT OUT

Join a small group at your local church. Seek out mentorship from mature Christians or your pastor. Allow the Lord to guide you as you lean into the Word of God and grow in knowledge and faith.

Heavenly Father,

You are the perfector of my faith. Please help me serve and honor You with everything I say and do. My heart desires never to return to my old ways or be tempted to live in sin. Holy Spirit, guide me and give me strength to follow You.

In Jesus' Name, Amen

Identify behaviors, responses, or thought patterns that no longer work in your best, Godly interest.

Endnotes

1   Viola, Frank. "Rethinking Paul's Thorn in the Flesh." Beyond Evangelical, 24 Apr. 2012, https://frankviola.org/2012/04/24/paulsthorninthe-flesh/.

2   "Notable Quotes by Max Planck." *Famous Quotes - Inspirational Quotes To Fire You Up With Motivation, The Famous People*, https://quotes.thefamouspeople.com/max-planck-4977.php.

3   Hammond, McKinney Michelle, and Joel A. Brooks. The Unspoken Rules of Love: What Women Don't Know and Men Don't Tell You. Water-Brook Press, 2005.

4   Ibid.

5   "A Quote by Karl Barth." Goodreads, Goodreads, https://www.goodreads.com/quotes/1602-laughter-is-the-closest-thing-to-the-grace-of-god.

6   DiSalvo, David. "Six Science-Based Reasons Why Laughter Is the Best Medicine." Forbes, Forbes Magazine, 5 June 2017, https://www.forbes.com/sites/daviddisalvo/2017/06/05/six-science-based-reasons-why-laughter-is-the-best-medicine/?sh=52c0bfba7f04.

7   Caesar, Shirley. "This Joy That I Have." *Rise Up & Sing.* https://www.riseupandsing.org/songs/joy-i-have

8   George, Jim. *A Husband after God's Own Heart.* Harvest House, 2004.

9   Boom, Corrie Ten, et al. *The Hiding Place: The Triumphant True Story of Corrie Ten Boom.* Bantam, 1974.

10   Graham, Billy. "God Is the Giver and Source of Life." *Press-Reader.com - Digital Newspaper & Magazine Subscriptions, 11 Aug. 2020,* https://www.pressreader.com/usa/chattanooga-times-free-press/20200811/282024739615159.

11   Morrison, Dr. Jeanne, and Diana Meeks. "Health Topics." Sharecare, https://www.sharecare.com/health/pain-management.

12   "Samuel Chadwick Quotes." *Quoteslyfe.com,* 2023. Sun. 19 Mar. 2023. <https://www.quoteslyfe.com/quote/Compassion-costs-It-is-easy-enough-to-1038989>.

13   Contributors, iBelieve. "Patience Is a Virtue: 6 Ways to Grow in This Fruit of the Spirit." IBelieve.com, Salem Web Network, 13 Mar. 2018, https://www.ibelieve.com/faith/patience-is-a-virtue-6-ways-to-grow-in-this-fruit-of-the-spirit.html.

14   Taylor, Howard, and Geraldine Taylor. Hudson Taylor's Spiritual Secret. Moody Publishers, 2009.

15   Lewis, Clive S. *Mere Christianity.* Macmillan, 1967.

16   "What Is the Difference between Wisdom and Knowledge?" *GotQuestions.org, 3 July 2015, https://www.gotquestions.org/wisdom-knowledge.html.*

17   Ralph Waldo Emerson, Society and Solitude, Courage. Quote reported in Hoyt's New Cyclopedia Of Practical Quotations (1922), p. 419-23

18   GotQuestions.org. "What does Paul mean when he says he is "forgetting those things which are behind" (Philippians 3:13)?" Got Questions, 17 October 2022, https://www.gotquestions.org/forgetting-those-things-which-are-behind.html. Accessed 9 March 2023.

19   Warren, Rick. *The Purpose Driven Life: What on Earth Am I Here for? Zondervan, 2021.*

20   *Healthy, Wealthy, and Wise: Principals for Successful Living from the Life of Benjamin Franklin. Summit Group, 1993.*

21   Piper, John. "Hope for Children from Dysfunctional Families." *Desiring God, 12 Apr. 2021,* https://www.desiringgod.org/interviews/hope-for-children-from-dysfunctional-families.

22   Indeed Editorial Team. "Accountable vs. Responsible: What's the Difference? (with Examples)." *Indeed, 10 Mar. 2023, https://www.indeed.com/career-advice/career-development/accountable-vs-responsible.*

23   "Stop Shrinking Yourself to Fit Places- Furaha Joyce Quotes: Likeable Quotes, Picture Quotes, Quotes." Pinterest, 11 Sept. 2021, https://www.pinterest.com/pin/stop-shrinking-yourself-to-fit-places-furaha-joyce-quotes--353321533275921830/.

About the Author

Born and raised in Chicago, Carlos Rivera served in the Navy after high school. He worked for several Fortune 500 companies before founding the highly successful *Home Mortgage Depot*, where he was president for eight years before going into full-time ministry.

Carlos has overseen church plants in João Pessoa, Brazil, Accra, Ghana, and Santiago De Los Caballeros, Dominican Republic. He has also provided ministry training and mentorship to hundreds of pastors and leaders around the globe to ensure their churches will thrive as they reach their communities with the life-giving truth of the gospel.

Carlos Rivera is passionate about encouraging the church to get out of our four walls and into our communities to win the lost for Christ.

During COVID, Carlos' belief in the power of prayer inspired "Walking in the Spirit," a morning prayer and devotional gathering joined by people around the world, as well as a weekly podcast of the same name.

Carlos and his wife, Rosalinda, are Senior Pastors at *New Life Outreach Church* and the Executive Directors of *New Life for Adults and Youth*, headquartered in Richmond, Virginia. They are committed to helping young men and women with substance abuse or other life-controlling problems find hope and a future through the life-changing power of Jesus Christ.

Carlos continues to be invited to teach nationally and globally in countries such as Africa, Peru, Brazil, and the Dominican Republic. He also speaks at church conferences and is committed to helping people reach their God-given potential.

Carlos and Rosalinda have been happily married for over 27 years and have three wonderful children.

FOR BOOKING
INFORMATION
Call 804-276-6767